To Sieglinde,

                    " You

Instruct yourself, o

Or carry report. You are here to kneel
Where prayer has been valid. And prayer is more
Than an order of words, the conscious occupation
Of the praying mind, or the sound of the
                              voice praying. "

                    Little Gidding from Four Quartets.
                         T. S. Eliot.

Christmas 1964.

                    Margaret.

HE SENT LEANNESS

HE SENT
LEANNESS

BY

DAVID HEAD

A book of prayers
for the natural man

LONDON

EPWORTH PRESS

FIRST PUBLISHED IN 1959
REPRINTED 1959
REPRINTED 1962

© THE EPWORTH PRESS 1959

Book Steward
FRANK H. CUMBERS

PRINTED IN GREAT BRITAIN BY ROBERT MACLEHOSE AND CO. LTD
THE UNIVERSITY PRESS, GLASGOW

*To my former Principal and teacher
the Rev. R. Newton Flew, M.A., D.D.
naturally!*

Contents

They soon forgat his works;
They waited not for his counsel:
But lusted exceedingly in the wilderness,
And tempted God in the desert.
And he gave them their request;
But sent leanness into their soul.

PSALM 106^{13–15} (A.V.)

But the natural man receiveth not the things of the Spirit of God: for they are foolishness unto him: neither can he know them, because they are spiritually discerned.

I CORINTHIANS 2¹⁴ (A.V.)

The natural man neither fears nor loves God.

JOHN WESLEY

The Prayer of the Author

Grant, I beseech Thee,

that all who read this book may be conscious of the deep spiritual insight of the writer;

that the sale of this book may result in a nice little nest-egg, even after income-tax has been deducted;

that copies of this book, nicely bound, may make an impressive sight in the study, on the bookshelf which is level with the eye;

that amid all the congratulatory applause, the writer may remain conspicuously humble.

PREFACES

Note

*to any gentlewoman who, misled by the
title, expects to find in this book advice for
the reduction of the figure*

I am very sorry. You won't.

Preface
for the natural man

It is one of the marks of the natural man that he
never reads prefaces unless he himself is mentioned
as having typed the manuscript, drawn up the index,
or been patient with the author's literary fervour and
personal neglect.

That being so, only my wife will read this page,
and while I apologize to her for putting her under
the category of 'natural man', I thank her for being
such a charmingly natural woman.

There are several messages I should like to send to
her, but this is hardly the time and place. Hardly the
place, anyway. She knows what anniversary we are
celebrating today. Indeed, she had to remind me.

Ibadan & Radcliffe-on-Trent

11

Preface

for the extra-literary natural man

In spite of an author's scepticism, there are in fact a few natural men who read the preface of a book and very little else. These are they who only read books in libraries and bookshops, and have little time to read the book itself.

To save them any embarrassment which might arise through staying three days in a bookshop without buying anything, I have decided to relegate the unusually long preface to the back of the book, where there is more room anyway. Here it becomes what may be termed a 'Postback'.

In spite of the inconveniences, we think the natural man should read it. We think he will like it. After all, we feel fairly certain that he is used to long Prefaces (though I am not quite shaw). There is a second reason: it is all about himself.

Preface
for the spiritual man

As the truly spiritual man will probably be too modest to read anything addressed to spiritual men, we have no doubt that this is the preface that will be read by natural men. To such we say: Go ahead and browse. Let us tell you one thing about yourself first. You are a man with a theology. Every man has some thoughts about God. They may be true or false, or more likely a complicated mixture — we hesitate to say muddle — of both. They are bound to be hopelessly inadequate. They may be making you a happier and better man. They may stand like a massive wall between you and your true freedom and joy.

But do not only be content to have thoughts. Switch the heart on, and turn them into prayers. If this book puts any man off his prayers, let the author's neck change the collar for the millstone. Prayers can be silly, harmful, childish, misguided, and selfish, but a personality that reaches out toward God is never cast out. It is alway better to pray foolishly than not at all, so long as you always remember that God is not in your pocket. Remember that the God toward whom you turn your thoughts must always be the Unknown God. Did you really think you could contain Him in your mind? Let the words 'through

13

Jesus Christ our Lord' be neither a lucky charm, nor a meaningless convention, nor a hint to the organist that it is time to sing the Amen, but a sieve through which you desire to pass all your thoughts and emotions and desires. The two things about God that matter supremely are that He is a living God, and that He is very much like Jesus.

If, however, there are 'spiritual men' among us, who might even suppose that there is actually something to be learnt from the following pages, let us make a bargain with them. We permit you to join the natural man in his prayers, only on the following strict conditions:

(1) that you do not hurry over any prayer, however short;

(2) that you may laugh, but not scoff;

(3) that any thoughts which arise in you will all be turned to yourself, and none to others (not even the wife);

(4) that you ask yourself about any prayer,
 (*a*) what is wrong here, if anything?
 (*b*) what thoughts about God and man are behind this prayer?
 (*c*) when did I last pray a prayer like this?
 (*d*) how can this prayer be brought into the truth?

(5) that you will pray more and not less, and think more about what you pray, and flood the subconscious with positive thoughts of truth by regular, quiet meditation;

(6) that you will be more concerned about God than about your thoughts of God, more concerned with His life than your opinions, more concerned with what He offers than your efforts to think well or do good;

(7) that you are content to be natural and supernatural, never unnatural; that you will seek to be sanctified, not sanctimonious.

Are we agreed? Then you may read on.

Preface

for any animal that chances to paw this book

Paws off, please! There is little appetizing in these pages, and the glue of the binding is distinctly unpleasant.

However, you may be curious about this book, particularly as leanness reminds one of Pharaoh's kine, and has other unfortunate associations.

This is a book of prayers which men pray, though they do not always realize it. It has one great omission, which few apart from four-footeds like you would notice. There is little about nature.

Now the natural man has a lot to do with nature. He keeps pets and cattle. He farms the land, and sometimes has strange feelings of awe and peace in the face of the power and beauty of the natural order. Indeed, he frequently visits the parks rather than the pews, and thinks he is nearer to God's heart in a garden than anywhere else on earth including the communion rail.

What he does not know is that he is the priest of nature, that God has appointed him not only nature's crown, but nature's spokesman. He is to make the unceasing praise of nature articulate. The lark may not know that he is praising God in his melodious rapture, but man knows Sometimes we suspect that the lark knows too, but not as man knows.

16

Now, it is only the spiritual man who understands nature. He knows his relation to nature, and he accepts his responsibility to nature. He may, during the intense emotional stress of conversion, have little 'use' for nature, but he will sooner or later come to appreciate that

> *something lives in every hue,*
> *Christless eyes have never seen*

Did not von Hügel warn us that we need two conversions, one 'to grace', and one 'to nature'? In the meantime, the natural man digs his garden, and praises God in his toil if not in his heart. One day he too may join the chorus of nature's priests in their refrain: 'Let everything that hath breath, praise the Lord.' In the meantime, he tolerates the zoo and the hunt, and makes nothing of the prophecy that the wolf shall lie down with the lamb.

Forgive us men. We have less courage, less pleasure, less spontaneity than you. But God seems to have some special plan for this strange creature man. If only he were a little less often on his hind legs, and a little more often on his knees!

THE NATURAL MAN AT WORSHIP

A General Confession

I

Benevolent and easy-going Father:[1] we have occasionally been guilty of errors of judgement. We have lived under the deprivations of heredity and the disadvantages of environment. We have sometimes failed to act in accordance with common sense. We have done the best we could in the circumstances; And have been careful not to ignore the common standards of decency; And we are glad to think that we are fairly normal. Do thou, O Lord, deal lightly with our infrequent lapses. Be thy own sweet Self with those who admit they are not perfect; According to the unlimited tolerance which we have a right to expect from thee. And grant as an indulgent Parent that we may hereafter continue to live a harmless and happy life and keep our self-respect.

BOOK OF COMMON PRAYER (Altered)

[1] 'Why is it that he is in no dread of God? Because he is totally ignorant of him: If not saying in his heart, "There is no God"; ... yet, satisfying himself as well, to all Epicurean intents and purposes, by saying, "God is merciful"; confounding and swallowing up all at once in that unwieldy idea of mercy all his holiness and essential hatred of sin; all his justice, wisdom, and truth.' — John Wesley, Sermon: 'The Spirit of Bondage and of Adoption', *Works*, V. 99–100.

Almighty Judge: we have lived far from thy ways like wild goats. We have on all occasions rebelliously followed our own inclinations. We have deliberately and shamelessly broken thy holy laws. We have never done anything we ought to have done; And we have done everything we ought not to have done; And we are utterly depraved. We desperately miserable offenders can only expect thy harsh judgement. We live obsessed with the unrelieved knowledge of our guilt. The thought of Jesus Christ does nothing except increase the depth of our shame. We have no right to expect anything hereafter except the intolerable burden of our unrighteousness, and the hell of our eternal disgrace.

BOOK OF COMMON PRAYER (Altered)

3

We are quite ready to admit that we have on occasions failed to live up to our highest standards, and we shall try to do a bit better in the New Year.

4

We confess that we have lost all our ideals, but congratulate ourselves that we have reached that stage of maturity which makes it possible to live without such adolescent encumbrances.

5

We have done wrong, but we hope nobody will find out.

A Litany

O God, we have considerable doubts in our minds about the way You are running the universe.
> *Is there any chance that You will show Your mercy to us, O Lord?*

We see all kinds of things in the world that do not please us.
> *Do you think You could do something about it, O God?*

The psychologists tell us that our nagging doubts about Your goodness burrow into the subconscious mind and spit poison.
> *Isn't this a bit unfair, O Lord?*

From a universe where things can be extremely unpleasant,
> *Deliver us, Good Lord.*

From everything that calls from us courage and endurance,
> *Deliver us, Good Lord.*

From all ignorance, insecurity, and uncertainty,
> *Deliver us, Good Lord.*

From all personal needs that give the love of others a chance to find expression,
> *Deliver us, Good Lord.*

From suffering the balloon of our pride to be pricked, from suffering the castle of our self-satisfaction to be attacked, from suffering the thunder of our egotism to be stilled,
Deliver us, Good Lord.

From all vicissitudes and deprivations that throw us back upon You,
Deliver us, Good Lord.

We sinners do hope against hope that You will pay just a little attention to our prayers; and that it may please You to get on with Your business, and do the best You can for us;
We beg You on our knees (as far as the pews will allow), O Lord.

That it may please You to bring good to us, and not evil, and that You will be on the side of light rather than darkness;
We beg You on our knees, O Lord.

That it may please You to rule and govern Your holy Church Universal in the right way;
We beg You on our knees, O Lord.

Hear us, O Lord.
Be Yourself, O Lord.

We citizens of the world do beseech You that the standard of living of our country may approximate more and more closely to that of the United States;
You can do all things, O God.

We sinners do pray that our national income may be enough to produce a sufficiency of nuclear weapons, maintain the Welfare State, and leave a little over for commonwealth countries;

You can do all things, O God.

We miserable owners of increasingly luxurious cars, and ever-expanding television screens, do most humbly pray for that two-thirds of the world's population which is under-nourished;

You can do all things, O God.

We who seek to maintain a shaky civilization do pray most earnestly that the countries which suffer exploitation may not be angry with the exploiters, that the hungry may not harbour resentment against those who have food, that the down-trodden may take it patiently, that nations with empty larders may prefer starvation to communism, that the 'have not' countries may rejoice in the prosperity of those that have, and that all people who have been deeply insulted and despised may have short memories;

You can do all things, O God.

We who prosper through the work and patience of others pray that we may have the sense not to drive them too far;

You can do all things, O God.

We pray that our statesmen may do everything they can to promote peace, so long as our own national history and honour and pride and prosperity and superiority and sovereignty are maintained;

You can do all things, O God.

That the sick may be visited, the prisoner cared for, the refugee rehabilitated, the naked clothed, the orphan housed, and that we may be allowed to enjoy our own firesides, evening by evening, in peace;
You can do all things, O God.

O Son of God, we beg, we beseech, we supplicate, we petition, we implore You to hear us.
Lord, be good to us.
Christ, make things easy for us.
Lord, deliver us from the necessity of doing anything.

Let us pray

O God, You see that we live in a world of toil and travail, with the vague possibility that there might be something worth while at the end of it. We pray You to take from man the embarrassing gift of free-will that made possible the Fall, and makes possible the fall of everyman. Grant that we may all become unselfconscious parts of one vast, universal factory, where everything works by automation, according to the press-button activity of the One Divine Will.
O Lord, arise. Give up this awful experiment of making men like Christ.

O God, we have heard all kinds of things about waters parting, and manna falling, and the sun standing still, and fire descending on altars.
O Lord, nothing like this seems to happen any more, and although we see some sense in the uniformity of Nature, we wish You could still see Your way to

24

making an occasional exception when it affects us personally.

Don't let anyone say nasty things about us.
May all men speak well of us.

Don't let our witness for Christ make things awkward for us.
Let it be the aim of our life not to do anybody any harm.

Don't let our neighbours go one better than us.
Keep us respectable, whatever our thoughts are, O Lord.

Almighty God, there are so many uncertain factors in life. We pray that we may be a little more certain of You. We ask You to be good to us sometimes, to bless us now and again, to give us in some small way an occasional release from our doubts and worries. We believe there are times, even if not frequent, when we deserve Your blessing. Do not let us down. *Amen.*

Private prayers before Public Worship

(with the head bowed and back bent, according to the uncomfortable tradition of Nonconformist piety)

I

So I'm not late after all thank goodness I was afraid when I saw Mrs Goodbody in front of me that I was all behind she is notorious for arriving during the last verse of the first hymn if only I hadn't been quite so long out with the dog everything would have been all right and then what with getting home late from the dance last night the shoes hadn't been cleaned and then I discovered I hadn't anything under half-a-crown for the collection and after all that Jack coughed up for the drinks last night I couldn't possibly put in all that it's funny how impossible it is to ask the nextdoor for change without being caught up in conversation about the weather and baby's teeth and what Mrs Green thought Mrs Brown said to Mrs Black I wonder if Mrs Brown really said such a thing I wouldn't put it past her anyway I've managed to get here on time even if the choir are just going to begin after all it does look so irreverent to come rushing into church after everything has started. *Amen.*

Dear Sieglinde,

I send you this because I know that you are able to laugh at yourself: I send it because I know that you embark upon the Divine Conversation, and in so doing may hear yourself passing remarks like these; finally, I send you this because I know that you have a Companion in your laughter who can change the lame echoes of these prayers.

Happy reading!

Love,
Margaret.

P.T.O.

Hazards of living at Whitefields!
See P. 27 Nº 3!

O God, I hope the sermon doesn't last more than fifteen minutes.

Please Lord, grant that I did turn the oven down.

If I'd known he was preaching, I'd have come this evening instead.

Lord, give us all a nice feeling this morning. May Thy special blessing be with those who will be active in this service while the rest of us sit still and listen. We pray that we may enjoy the preliminaries, and that the sermon may give us all a glow. I know I have offended at least two people this week with my quick temper, but please do not let the thought of that intrude upon this spiritual feast. Praise God. *Amen.*

JESUS AND THE NATURAL MAN

Prayers not prayed

(*a*) Solomon:
    For myself:
        Long life,
        and riches,
        and the life of my enemies.

I KINGS 3[11]

(*b*) A greater than Solomon:
    Take away this cup from me, Amen.

MARK 14[36]

    Father, save me from this hour.

JOHN 12[27]

    Take them out of the world.

JOHN 17[15]

No for an answer

Peter
    Depart from me, for I am a sinful man, O Lord.
    Be it far from thee, Lord: this shall not be unto
        thee.
    Let us make three tabernacles; one for thee, and
        one for Moses, and one for Elijah.
    Thou shalt never wash my feet.
    Lord, and what shall this man do?

James and John

Lord, wilt thou that we command fire to come down from heaven, and consume them, even as Elias did?

Grant unto us that we may sit, one on thy right hand, and one on thy left, in thy glory.

The disciples

Lord, wilt thou at this time restore again the kingdom to Israel?

Those that passed by, also the chief priests, with scribes and elders

Thou that destroyest the temple, and buildest it in three days, save thyself.

If thou be the Son of God, come down from the cross.

If he be the King of Israel, let him now come down from the cross, and we will believe him.

He trusted in God; let him deliver him now, if he will have him: for he said, I am the Son of God.

A demon

What have I to do with thee, Jesus, thou Son of the most high God? I adjure thee, by God, that thou torment me not.

The devil

If thou be the Son of God, command that these stones be made bread.

If thou be the Son of God, cast thyself down.

All these things will I give thee, if thou wilt fall
down and worship me.
(From LUKE 5⁸, MATTHEW 16²², MARK 9⁵,
JOHN 14⁸, 21²¹
LUKE 9⁵⁴, MARK 10³⁷
ACTS 1⁶
MATTHEW 27³⁹⁻⁴³
MARK 5⁷
MATTHEW 4³, ⁶, ⁹)

'The men which thou gavest me'
JOHN 17

'They are not of the world'
God, I thank thee, that I am not as other men are,
extortioners, unjust, adulterers, or even as this
publican.

I fast twice in the week, I give tithes of all that I
possess.
LUKE 18¹¹⁻¹²

'They are in the world'
Lord, let me be all things to all men, that I may
have the good opinion of all. May I never upset
people, or say things they are likely to disagree with.
May I pat everyone on the back without distinction.
May I always be ready to adapt my principles, so as
never to offend. So may I spread a little happiness
as I pass along.

'I sent them into the world'
Lord, make me a soul-winner to the exclusion of
all else. Let all men feel uncomfortable in my

presence. Deliver me from the temptation to read novels, enjoy music, stand and stare. Let me never waste time in unevangelistic conversation. Let me not be slow to tell others their faults. Deliver me from the weary process of getting to know people and offering friendship. May every week add more jewels to my crown.

THE RESPONSE OF THE
NATURAL MAN

Thou Fool

Psalm 10, verse 11
> God has forgotten,
> He has hidden His face, He will never see it.

Psalm 10, verse 13
> Thou wilt not call to account.

Psalm 59, verse 7
> Who will hear us?

Psalm 64, verse 5
> Who can see us?
> Who can search out our crimes?

Psalm 73, verse 11
> How can God know?
> Is there knowledge in the Most High?

Man answers the call of God

(a) *Don't come near me*
> I heard thy voice in the garden,
> and I was afraid, ...
> and I hid myself.

GENESIS 3¹⁰

(b) *It wasn't my fault*

And the man said, The woman whom thou
gavest to be with me, she gave me of the tree
and I did eat.

And the woman said, The serpent beguiled me,
and I did eat.

GENESIS 3[12-13]

(c) *I'm doing all right*

Soul, thou hast much goods laid up for many
years; take thine ease, eat, drink, and be
merry.

I am rich, and increased with goods, and have
need of nothing.

LUKE 12[19]   REVELATION 3[17]

(d) *One of these days*

Lord, I have every intention of repenting before
I die.[1]

---

[1] Compare St Augustine:
'There was nothing I could reply when You called me:
"Rise, thou that sleepest and arise from the dead: and
Christ shall enlighten thee"; and whereas You showed me
by every evidence that Your words were true, there was
simply nothing I could answer save only laggard lazy words:

Soon,

Quite soon,

Give me just a little while.

But "soon" and "quite soon" did not mean any particular
time; and "just a little while" went on for quite a long
while.'   *Confessions,* trans. F. J. SHEED

(e) *I don't need church*
>   Lord, Thou knowest I am on the side of the
>   angels, but don't ask me to worship with them.

(f) *A prayer for Ataraxia*[1]
>   O Lord, who dost promise us heaven as a place
>   of rest and quiet, grant that nothing may
>   upset me today.

>   Let me hear the shout of laughter and the cry of
>   pain without getting worked up. Let me
>   guard the citadel of my emotions from all
>   intruding disturbances. Let me avoid at all
>   costs the conversation that shakes like an
>   earthquake the foundations of my mind.

>   Let me view all things with calm detachment
>   from a superior height. Let my pity be a
>   controlled thing, my love a calculated thing,
>   my joy without crescendos, and my meekness
>   without muscle.

>   Let the teaching of Christ bring me consolation,
>   not challenge. Let familiarity with the story
>   of the Cross guard me from stress and shame.

See also John Wesley:
'He is secure because he is utterly ignorant of himself.
Hence he talks of "repenting by and by"; he does not
indeed exactly know when, but some time or other before
he dies; taking it for granted that this is quite in his own
power.' — Sermon, 'The Spirit of Bondage and of Adoption', *Works,* V.100.

[1] A virtue at which the Stoics and Epicureans aimed. It
has been defined as 'freedom from disturbing emotions'.

Help me to be still and know that I am good.
Lord, in Thy mercy, grant me death not life, for
 life is uneasy motion, and death has no
 surprises.

Prayers of pious intention

1

If God will be with me,
    and will keep me in this way that I go,
    and will give me bread to eat,
    and raiment to put on,
        so that I come again to my father's house
            in peace;
then shall the Lord be my God,
    and this stone, which I have set for a pillar, shall
    be God's house:
    and of all that thou shalt give me I will surely
    give the tenth unto thee.

GENESIS 28$^{20-22}$

2

O Lord, if I can get away with it this time, I
promise I'll never steal again.

3

Dear Lord, I really should like to attend the
weekly Fellowship meeting, but there is such a good
programme on the Telly every Thursday evening.

O Lord, so long as the weather is reasonably fine,

> so long as I have no visitors,
>
> so long as nobody asks me to do any work,
>
> so long as I can sit in the back pew but one on the left,
>
> so long as it isn't a local preacher planned,
>
> so long as they don't choose hymns I don't know,
>
> so long as my Joe is asked to recite at the Anniversary,
>
> so long as I can get home in time for the play,

I will honour Thee with my presence at Church whenever I feel like it.

Dear God, if it were not for the war and Philip's illness, I should like to believe in Thee.

So long as things go smoothly with me, I promise never to neglect to remove my hat to a passing funeral. [1]

[1] The story is told of Voltaire, that he bared his head when a funeral went by. His friend said: 'I thought you didn't believe in God.' He replied: 'We acknowledge each other, though we aren't on speaking terms.'

THE NATURAL MAN PLEADS
AND INTERCEDES

All sorts and conditions of men

1
A natural man (male)

I thank Thee that it is I, and not my wife, who wears the trousers.[1]

2
A natural blonde

Keep my hair a crown of glory that fadeth not away.

3
A born actor

For once in my life, let me be natural.

4
An overworked parson

May I fulfil all the duties that I see, but do not let me see too many.

5
A very natural genius

Lord, can I ever forgive Thee that I am not as other men are?

[1] Compare the Jewish benediction: 'Blessed art thou, O Lord our God, King of the universe, who hast not made me a woman.'

A natural scientist

Why is it, O God, that I cannot share the faith of my father? He holds a simple trust, and to him this world is Thy world. But although I stand in humility before the immensity of the galaxies, I cannot see Thee as lord of the heavens.

Men are but specks of dust on an utterly insignificant planet. What is man, that Thou art mindful of him? The psalmist's answer finds no echo in my heart.

How much the laboratory shows that is wonderful! The delicate balance of the human body and mind; the instinct of birds; the fascinating structure of each flower; the intricacy of the molecule.

I feel something akin to awe as science year by year pushes back the frontiers of the natural world. But, but, I do not see Thee as Creator. Yet I must live and seek to be whole.

If science with all its perceptions and powers cannot lead me to Thyself, what other path is there?

7

A natural parent

O Lord, do not let William grow up too quickly. May he make no decisions without consulting me first. May he still find his greatest pleasure in my company. I know he is developing new interests, and making new friends, but I do want to share in every part of his life. Remind him constantly of all that he owes to his parents. Prevent him from growing too independent. And if he must have a girl, let it be that sweet little Cynthia Black.

8

A nature worshipper

Drat those ants!

9

A logician

How can I address Thee? To say that Thou art omniscient, omnipotent, and omnipresent is merely to stretch human terminology beyond bounds. Do these words mean everything — or nothing?

How can I call Thee Creator, when the idea of creation out of nothing confounds me utterly? How can I address Thee as Judge, when Thou hast neither courtroom, wig, nor jury?

Can I speak of Thee as Father? The word used of deity is barren and meaningless. Thou didst neither fertilize the seed from which I came, nor help to bring me up. Thou wast not the breadwinner of my family. It was another, who is truly called father, who didst provide me with the security of a home.

O God, whatever I say of Thee is bound to be false. Therefore I will say nothing.

I cannot find Thee by logical processes, therefore I will conclude that Thou canst not be found.

Thou art too great for human comprehension, therefore I will assume that Thou art so small as to be non-existent.

Thou canst not be described in human terms, therefore I reason that there is nothing to be described.

A pseudo-spiritual athlete

O God, who dwellest in eternity, how canst Thou be interested in the time of a hundred-yards race? As Thy word has put it, the race is not to the swift. We have been reminded also, by the Psalmist and Isaac Watts, that Thou dost not take delight in the legs of a man. Thou art far beyond such human interests. May my feet be dedicated only to hurrying to prayer meetings.

The Changing Scenes

I

Childhood

God bless Mummy and Daddy. (It was a bit mean sending me to bed before the really interesting grown-up telly.)

Bless Auntie Mary who came today. (It was decent of her to read my books, but she might have given me a bigger bar of chocolate.)

Bless my friends. (I like Johnny, but I can't stick that Gerald Green, and I'll get even with him for pinching my ball.)

Thank You for a lovely day. (Apart from those awful sums that never come right.)

Make me a good boy. (I will try to be, so long as I can have my own way always.)

Make my sister Joan better. (It's only a bad cough, and she always gets over it in a day or two.)

Keep us safe this night. (Don't let those awful black shadows get at me.)

I do love You, Jesus, almost as much as I love my teddy bear.

2
Adolescence

Nobody understands me, and it is hard to believe that You do.

Since the world's future is too terrible to contemplate, let us find our consolation in jeering and jiving, rocking and rolling.

In spite of the mess made by all previous generations, may we build the Kingdom of God on earth through scientific knowledge and technical skill.

3
Relations, Neighbours, Friends, and Enemies

I pray for the relations with whom I have been encumbered. Thou knowest that they are a pretty rum lot. I should hardly have chosen a single one of them. Help me to find some good in them, however difficult a job that may be. Don't let me see too much of any of them. Let the occasional duty visits be brief and bearable. Thou understandest that I have no time to write to them, but let the expensive and unavoidable Christmas Card express my sincere good wishes.

Lord, what selfish, thoughtless, jealous, difficult and presumptuous people most of my neighbours are. May I be rewarded for my patience with them, by finding that they are all of use to me.

God save me from my friends.[1]

I thank Thee for my friends, so sweet and kind, so much wiser and stronger than I. I don't deserve a single one of them. Make me a doormat for their feet, a willing target for their wit, a sponge for their good advice, a trumpet for their interesting deeds. They must think a great deal of me, or they would not be so determined to rule my life for me. Make me humble and grateful.

May I always have someone I can help, for the sake of my self-esteem.

God forgive him, for I never will.

(A clerk whose afternoon at the test-match has been refused)
Thou knowest the cold heart of my boss. Lord, make it hot for him.

4

Engagement and Marriage

May we find marriage the end of all our problems, and live happily ever after.

May he have no secrets, and never discover mine.

May she be always useful and always beautiful, full of interesting conversation, witty in private and sparkling in public, blind to my faults, tolerant with my follies, never weary, never demanding, enjoying

[1] This is attributed to Marshal de Villars, as he took leave of Louis XIV. He added: 'I can protect myself from my enemies.'

her own company when necessary, not getting too involved with female friends, performing miracles with her house-keeping allowance, and always grateful that I married her.

5
At Home and Abroad

Bless all foreigners, but don't let them come to live next door.

Bless all natives in foreign parts, and keep them there.

Lord, I know it is the task of the Church to preach the Gospel. But do we have to cross thousands of miles of ocean or sky to do it? Thou knowest that there is plenty to do in our own town, even in our own street. Deliver us from straining our eyes to see some special need at the ends of the earth, while ignoring the responsibilities under our noses. Forgive the longsightedness that gets the nearer tasks out of focus. Provide men and money for all our needs at home. And don't call my son to be a missionary.

(A Christian worker overseas)
O God, help all those among whom I work to be proficient at English.

(A grave white man)
Lord, help me not to lose my temper with my cook-steward more than once a week. He deserved it today — he knows quite well that we do not pour

43

hot custard on to spaghetti. May he be more grateful. After all, he gets six pound a month, and it is his own fault that he has eight children and is ambitious about their education. Make him honest, so that our sugar bill is reduced. Keep him sober at all times, to prevent a recurrence of that dreadful scene at our drinking-party last night at 1.30 a.m. And make a good Christian of him, even if he can never be spared to go to Church on Sundays.

6

In face of suffering

O God, don't let me die.[1]

I've always lived a decent life. What have I done to deserve this?

I knew when I went under that ladder that something would happen.

O Lord, let my temperature go down before Saturday, but not too long before.

Help my tooth-ache to go, without having to trouble the poor, overworked dentist.

I thank Thee that I had more gall-stones than Mrs Peters.

Master, carest thou not that we perish?

If thou canst do anything. . . .

[1] It is said of the Cornish evangelist, Billy Bray, that while waiting with his fellow workers to begin his shift in the tin mine, he prayed: 'Lord, if any have to die this day, let it be me, for I am ready.'

7

Old Age

Surely at my age, I can do what I like![1]

8

In face of death

I suppose I've nothing to be scared of, but I can't help wishing I'd put a little more in the collection plate last time I went to Church.

I thank Thee that the family are around me now. It has always taken a death in the family to bring us together. They have come a bit too early this time, and it will be a pleasure to keep them waiting. Sister Jessie would like to have been here today, but she went first, as I expected she would. Too many pills! My greatest consolation now is that I am leaving more money than she did. Harry's here, of course, back from the ends of the earth to see me go. He won't get a penny of mine. Cousin Mabel I did not expect. I have not seen her for fifteen years, since I offended her by telling her that she looked ten years older than her age. She still does, and I enjoyed telling her so yesterday. James, of course, now that he is gone all religious, is loving every minute of this. 'We'll meet in heaven, Auntie,' he said. I hope not!

[1] See A. J. Cronin, *The Keys of the Kingdom:* 'He entered the pro-cathedral, an echoing vastness of beauty and silence. . . . Undaunted, he marched toward the high altar. There he knelt and fiercely, with unshaken valour, prayed: "Oh Lord, for once — not Thy will, but mine, be done." '

And I shall try to keep out of the way of our late cousin the Rev. Ernest. It is bad enough to have to put up with parsons in the family, on earth. I shall avoid Aunt Freda, too. She ought never to have been allowed to marry into our family. Come to think of it, the only member of the family I have the slightest desire to meet in heaven is my precious ginger cat Cuddles.

No doubt, Lord, this is the moment to turn my mind to higher things. Thou knowest my absorbing business interests and my participation in serious golf over the years. Now I must lift my mind from earthly pursuits to the contemplation of the future. I always knew that this would one day be necessary. Now the time has come.

The only picture I have ever been given of heaven is of a garish city of gold and pearls, entirely lacking in decent taste. One gathers that the gold is strictly confined to the road surface, as no mention is made of a Stock Exchange or a Bank. I rather think that white robes and branches of trees also feature in the picture. The thought of myself half-dressed in the undignified act of waving a palm branch is quite intolerable.

Nor am I the least bit cheered by the thought of harps. My dear Matilda, who rejected my suit in 1900 for the sake of a common actor, was a competent harpist. To hear the plucking of the strings again can only bring regret and melancholy.

It appears then that my only source of anticipation

is the prospect of a heavenly choir. As a choir boy, before I entered the world of business, I was quite acceptable. Surely a man of my position is entitled to a leading role. Indeed, in view of my untiring activities in the cause of commerce, and my undoubted abilities in the sphere of finance, I have every reason to suppose that they will make me treasurer.

Lord, I am quite convinced that I shall not be at home in heaven. Is this all You have to offer?

Lord, I've been active all my life. This idea of eternal rest frightens me. The beatific something-or-other they talk about in sermons doesn't mean a thing to me. I shall be thoroughly miserable, if all I have to do is to gaze and gaze. Isn't there anything to *do* in heaven?

O God, Thy eternal City as men have described it seems unbearably cosmopolitan. There are some nations (which I will not at present specify), some denominations (which shall be nameless), one political party (Lord, Thou knowest), and many types of musicians (if such a word can be applied to them at all), with whom I could not possibly live. Could I, perhaps, have a quiet detached mansion on my own, with a few specified visitors for short periods?

Lord, the thought of being a ghost haunts me.

So this is the end of everything. At any rate I've always thought it would be. But life is so full of disappointments, that one hardly dares to count on oblivion.

9

In Memoriam

To the memory of our dear son,
   killed on the roads,
knocked down by a car
    driven by a sensuous drunk.

THY WILL BE DONE

being an examination of the sub-title of this book,
addressed to all who have persevered this far

(a) That 'natural man' does not mean 'animal man'

This is a book of prayers for the natural man.
The 'natural man' takes some defining. What does
he look like? He is not simply 'animal man', for no
man is simply an animal, even in his most beastly
moments. If anyone doubts this, feeling that a theory
of evolution and a look at persons as they are provide
conclusive evidence of the animal nature of man,
there is an answer.

We do not deny that at times, possessed by lust or
fear, a man's emotions and motions may seem in-
distinguishable from those of an animal. Even here
we must tread softly, not having consciously trans-
migrated into a wolf or a swan. Neither do we deny
that animals and men have a lot in common. The
monkey-house at the zoo can be a terrifying revelation. We see animals with conditioned reflexes,
instincts (whatever they are), powers of logic, a sense
of humour, mother love.

How like us! Yet the mind and experience of
man seems to have taken a new turn. It will be
time enough to revise our opinions about this when
we hear of a young animal committing suicide, or of a

man travelling through space in a dog-launched rocket.

We may take it farther. Whatever psychological language we adopt, we have to accept that there are whole regions of the personality outside the realm of consciousness. We assert that there are things here that make man distinctively man. Oh, but does not the elephant have a subconscious? It seems inevitable. Where else shall we locate his proverbial memory? And, furthermore, if we grant for a moment that a man's subconscious mind contains both sleeping tigers and sleeping princesses, the psychologist is much less aware of beauty than beast. Does not the content of this deep human mind, as it is tipped by the barrow-load into the casebook of the psycho-analyst, confirm the basic animal nature of man?

As a matter of fact, it does not, or more animals would need the help of psychotherapy to live normal lives. However hard to define, man's make-up has a uniqueness which gives him a subtle superiority to stronger brutes than himself, opening up for him problems, and joys, and discoveries, and powers which make him not only a super-animal but a 'peculiar creature'. Man's outward behaviour should be enough to convince us. To say that men behave like beasts is always unfair to the beasts. Beasts never behave like beasts!

(b) That 'natural man' is neither divine nor devilish

We conclude that 'animal man' does not exist. There ain't no such animal. Whether he does or not, the phrase 'natural man' as used in biblical writings (and it comes into the language straight out of the Authorized Version) does not refer to him. How could it? The undeviating witness of the Jewish Scriptures, and of the New Testament writings which crown them, is that however dusty man may appear, God has breathed into his nostrils the breath of life.

There is the further point, that his breath has gone bad. Was this through eating overripe apples, or inhaling the smoke of hell? Disobedience, anyway. The clothes of his manhood were tailored for royalty, but his heavenly pants have become more holey than holy, whether through climbing forbidden trees, or by too many self-satisfied wriggles on the seat of the scornful. When Saint Paul speaks of the natural man, he accepts as self-evident that mankind is the core of a rebellious universe.

Does this mean, then, that 'natural man' is godless man? That is the sort of phrase that causes endless confusion. Is man-in-rebellion completely out of touch with the divine life? Those under the influence of Dr Karl Barth might say so, but they have also inherited from him a strong doctrine of creation. It depends what you mean.

There have always been those in the Church who have been most at home with the doctrine of Creation that man is made in the image of God, however much that image is distorted. Primitive man has a deep sense of awe and worship, far deeper apparently than that found in many Christian congregations today. Dr Nels Ferré begins his book *Strengthening*

51

the Spiritual Life by quoting Mother Alice Kaholu-
oluna of Hawaii:

'Before the missionaries came, my people used to
sit outside their temples for a long time meditating
and preparing themselves before entering. Then
they would virtually creep to the altar to offer their
petition and afterwards would again sit a long time
outside, this time to "breathe life" into their prayers.
The Christians, when they came, just got up, uttered
a few sentences, said Amen and were done. For that
reason my people call them haolis, "without breath",
or those who fail to breathe life into their prayers.'

It seems as though we who are invited to approach
the throne with boldness misinterpret this to mean
that we may come with our hands in our pockets.
As for primitive man, there is much evidence that he,
like the sophisticated Greeks of old, can look beyond
the familiar gods to the god who has no dealings
with charm or shrine, who rather stands aloof as the
transcendent One. Is there not a light that lighteth
every man?

At the same time, the Church has always contained
those whose experience and reflection have illumi-
nated so brightly the doctrine of Redemption from
sin and evil, that Creation, if not banished into outer
darkness, has had to lurk in the shadows. Man
indeed becomes a god, but a self-appointed one. His
greatest idol is himself. Primitive and advanced
society abound with the smears of man's bloody
fingers. There is none righteous, no, not one.

Out of the tension between these two doctrines

comes the historical controversy, still heard in the contemporary scene, between 'liberal' and 'evangelical'. Here too we find the extremes of world-acceptance (which is not necessarily acceptance of the 'worldly') and world-denial, of full-blooded sacramentalism and austere asceticism. The earth is the Lord's and the fullness thereof, but come ye apart and be ye separate, and touch not the unclean thing. Here too is the differing emphasis laid upon the Incarnation and the Atonement. Some would also find here the essential difference between 'Catholic' and 'Protestant', but not those who believe in the Catholicity of Protestantism. Tied up with all this, though even more entangled, is the controversy about infant and believers' baptism.

Creation and Redemption — of course we must have both. If the natural man is not an animal grown too big for his boots, neither is he an angel or a devil — not even a fallen angel or a redeemed devil. Natural man is a flesh-and-blood creation, part of the space-time world, but drawing his life from somewhere else. He is an utterly dependent creature, who finds himself resenting his dependence; a paradoxical production, created by the One Only Will to have a will of his own; a concoction of fearful complexity, capable of flirting with angels or demons and doing both; a colossus standing astride the gulf between heaven and earth, and finding it distinctly uncomfortable.

(c) That 'natural man' is sleeping man

With this view of man, we see all his deep-rooted

sin and deprivation as off-centre, eccentric, and un-natural, foreign to his 'real' nature as the creature and child of God. We might then use the phrase 'natural man' of Adam ('the man') in his innocence, or we might use it uniquely of the one true representative of humanity, Jesus Christ ('Behold the man'). We are prevented from doing so, because the Bible uses the phrase in a quite different way. To this we turn.

In biblical writings, 'natural man' (*psychikos anthropos*) only occurs in one Pauline passage (1 Corinthians 2¹⁴). It is this comparison of the natural and the spiritual man which has established its usage. The *Revised Standard Version* translates '*psychikos*' by 'unspiritual'. The adjective only occurs again when Paul speaks about the 'natural body' (a completely different idea), and twice in the catholic epistles. James speaks of the wisdom that is 'earthly, *psychikos, devilish*' (3¹⁵). Jude (verse 19) speaks of those with ungodly lusts, who are '*psychikos*, not having the Spirit'. On both these occasions the Authorized Version translates with the word 'sensual'. To continue in the lecture room one moment longer — the adjective derives from a very common biblical word '*psyche*', which refers to the soul, or basic life, of man. It is this human life which stands over against God, and it is in this sense that our souls need saving. This idea of lost humanity is common enough throughout Scripture, whatever the words used.

If we ask what sort of person this natural man is, we find the biblical answers gathered into one fold by the Rev. John Wesley in his sermon on 'The

Spirit of Bondage and of Adoption'. In spite of all
appearances to the contrary, in spite of natural man's
happiness 'to dress, and visit, and talk, and eat, and
drink, and rise up to play', he is suffering from a
more-than-mild soporific:

'His soul is in a deep sleep: his spiritual senses are
not awake: they discern neither spiritual good nor
evil. . . . He is utterly ignorant of God, knowing
nothing concerning Him as he ought to know. He
is totally a stranger to the law of God, as to its true,
inward, spiritual meaning. He has no conception of
that evangelical holiness, without which no man shall
see the Lord; nor of the happiness which they only
find whose "life is hid with Christ in God". And,
for this very reason, because he is fast asleep, he is, in
some sense, at rest. Because he is blind, he is also
secure.'[1]

Wesley proceeds with acute psychological precision to describe the natural man in all his ways. A
depressing picture! No doubt we have all at some
time picked up a book of common ailments and
diseases, and immediately been introduced to our
own aches and pains, the aching back, the sore toe,
the creaking elbow, and been horrified at their chronic
significance. So we look at the natural man, and
recognize ourselves in a thousand particulars.

But have we not received the Lord? Have we not
believed and been baptized; or perhaps been baptized, and believed? Are we not, by divine grace,
joined to the members of Christ's lively Body the

[1] *Works,* V.99.

Church? Have we not received the Holy Spirit, and become spiritual men?

Wesley has a word for us in this same context. After describing minutely the 'natural man', the man 'under the law', and the man 'under grace', he continues: 'Perhaps one reason why so many think of themselves more highly than they ought to think, why they do not discern what state they are in, is, because these several states of soul are often mingled together, and in some measure meet in one and the same person.'[1] To put it mildly, we are not yet made perfect in love! The thoughts and emotions of our conscious mind, and the hidden movements of our unconscious mind, are not yet brought into captivity to Christ. We are still being changed into the same image, from glory to glory. We are servants with a rebel bias. We are children with a slavish mentality. We are the redeemed with our shackles still dangling. We are justified, but we sin. We are saved and being saved, by grace, through faith. All this may be an explanation; it must never become an excuse. Be ye perfect!

(d) That prayer is an activity of the 'natural man'

Such then is the natural man, an unconscious rebel, building his house with technical precision on the edge of the precipice, having 'no light in the things of God'. Does such a man pray? The more respectable of the species will certainly take prayers upon their lips from time to time, if only to the extent of

[1] *Works*, V.109.

saying prayers in Church on Remembrance Sunday, or singing 'Abide with me', toffee-in-mouth, before the kick-off. Does the natural man pray with the heart? Surely he does, in moments of ecstasy or emergency? The bomber pilot, the miner's wife, the new-made mother, the arctic explorer, the exam-burdened scholar all know something of spontaneous prayer. But we must face the fact also, that when the natural man prays, he is talking in his sleep!

Here is a last quotation from Wesley. Still writing of the man in the 'natural' state, he says:

'A man may be of a compassionate and a benevolent temper; he may be affable, courteous, generous, friendly; he may have some degree of meekness, patience, temperance, and of many other moral virtues.... He may abstain from much evil; perhaps from all that is grossly contrary to justice, mercy, or truth. He may do much good, may feed the hungry, clothe the naked, relieve the widow and fatherless. *He may attend public worship, use prayer in private, read many books of devotion*; and yet, for all this, he may be a mere natural man, knowing neither himself nor God; equally a stranger to the spirit of fear and to that of love; having neither repented, nor believed the gospel.... Beware then, thou who art called by the name of Christ, that thou come not short of the mark of thy high calling. Beware thou rest not ... in a natural state, with too many that are accounted *good Christians*.'[1]

[1] Ibid. p. 110.

Let it be said that, while those first italics have been added, the second italics are Wesley's own. He would address us. Must we think of ourselves, at best, as those in whom 'the several states of soul are mingled together'? Let us examine ourselves then.

We 'good Christians', how do we pray? Are we spiritually awake in all our conscious intercourse with God? Must we not confess that our petitions, and thanksgivings (or lack of them), and even our praises, are coloured by the unconverted motions of our deep minds. Let us not for a moment scoff at the childish stammerings of 'those who know nothing as they ought to know', when we ourselves, we spiritual men, allow our fears and doubts and darling lusts to contaminate our prayers. In the first place, our prayers, if they are supplications of the heart and not conventional murmurings, reveal immediately *what we really believe about God.* We speak as though He were deaf, as though He needed encouragement, as though He needed to be won to the side of the angels, as though He were almighty in the sense of pushing people around at will, as though He were too small, or too lazy, or too full of Himself. It is not the inadequacy of our words that matters. Concise prayers and uplifting expressions are to help us, not God. God is in heaven, and thou on earth; we do not have to pretend we are anywhere else. What is subtly devastating is that our prayers are expressions of blasphemous distortions, and imply a God who is hardly worth knowing. We form our own image of God, and bow down to it, and inevitably become like it. Come forward, then, the man who believes in prayer but not in theology!

In the second place, our prayers reveal *what we really want*. We need not think to draw the wool over the divine eyes at this point. We are taught that God knows what we need. Equally, He knows what we want. All Christian prayer, however expressed, includes the honest attempt to find out what God wants. We forget that there lies our entire blessing. But we also have wills which may be anything from weak to high-handed. Says James in his letter: 'Ye ask, and receive not, because ye ask amiss, that ye may consume it upon your lusts.' How far have we travelled from the dominant pagan desires: What shall we drink? What shall we wear? What can we get out of this? In such circumstances, it is a great mercy when we receive not.

Life, however, is so constituted, that many things we deeply desire we get. Our personalities and possibilities are moulded by the act of asking. 'Take what you want, and pay for it, says God'; so runs the Spanish proverb. In this we may see the inexorable judgement of God's love. Many of our most futile prayers are attempts to dodge the divinely established fact that we reap what we sow. In the passage of Scripture which gives the title to this book, we read of the Israelites in the wilderness. It was, no doubt, a painful, bitter experience, especially after the false security of slavery. The trouble was, the Psalmist reflects, that in admittedly uncomfortable circumstances, the wanderers cried out to their God for

drink, and food, and especially meat (Numbers 11⁴).
Indeed, they made the provision of these things the
ultimate test of God's Presence and Call: 'Is the Lord
among us, or not?' (Exodus 17⁷). So tempted, God
can only reveal His active concern in righteous wrath:

> 'And he gave them their request;
> But sent leanness into their soul.'

So we have two things to ask: 'What is God like?'
and 'What do we really want of Him?' Perhaps it is
dawning upon us that these two questions are more
closely linked than we thought. For when all is said
and done, God has only one gift for us — Himself.
And He is both known in Christ, and given in Christ.
All things are yours, and you are Christ's, and
Christ is God's.

This book may show us how we pray. It is only
the Spirit of God who can show us how we ought to
pray, He who Himself maketh intercession for us
with groanings that cannot be uttered, He who
maketh intercession for the saints according to the
will of God.

EPILOGUE

(from ISAIAH 25¹⁶ PSALM 36^{7–9} EPHESIANS 3^{14–21}
  LUKE 11¹)

From the uttermost part of the earth have we heard songs, even glory to the righteous. But I said, My leanness, my leanness, woe unto me!

How excellent is thy lovingkindness, O God! Therefore the children of men put their trust under the shadow of thy wings.

They shall be abundantly satisfied with the fatness of thy house; And thou shalt make them drink of the river of thy pleasures.

For with thee is the fountain of life: In thy light shall we see light.

For this cause I bow my knees unto the Father of our Lord Jesus Christ, of whom the whole family in heaven and earth is named,

that he would grant you, according to the riches of his glory, to be strengthened with might by his Spirit in the inner man;

that Christ may dwell in your hearts by faith;

that ye, being rooted and grounded in love, may be able to comprehend with all saints what is the breadth and depth, and length, and height;

and to know the love of Christ, which passeth knowledge,

that ye might be filled with all the fullness of God.

Now unto him that is able to do
    exceeding abundantly
    above all that we ask or think,
    according to the power that worketh in us,
unto him be glory
in the church by Christ Jesus
throughout all ages, world without end. *Amen.*

LORD, TEACH US TO PRAY